TOP 30 SECTORS CREATING MOST NON-TECHNOLOGY JOBS THE NEXT 10 YEARS

Stephan S. Sunn

Davidson Global & Co.

CONTENTS

PREFACE

In this fully blown technological world, it is also very important to point out that this expansion goes hand in glove with the extension of jobs associated with no technology. These are offering very crucial support to emerging fields like Artificial Intelligence and Clean Energy. Such roles involve both traditional and evolving sectors: from energy infrastructure designed to power new AI developments to food production and agriculture, which remain foundational to any thriving society.

In this regard, non-technological careers have obtained even more importance today, showing their resistance and value for the performance of basic functions that provide for further growth. For instance, employment in sustainable agriculture would guarantee food security for all while contributing to environmental health a concern for all industries. These careers put food on the table and bring stability and a sense of purpose to one's life, as they offer young people meaningful and dynamic careers without necessarily having to pursue technical fields.

This book acts as a navigator toward the increasingly exciting opportunities awaiting one outside the realm of technology and serves as a guide toward the best sectors that are likely to provide nontechnical job growth over the decade. Identifying various job segments essential for sustainable and prosperous future development, away from digital confines, this work underlines emphatically that the vocation of non-technology is in no way less relevant to plotting the course toward a sustainable, prosperous future for anyone planning a fulfilling professional life.

CHAPTER 1: THE FUTURE OF WORK

A Shifting Job Landscape In A Tech-Driven World

Technology seems to have become the synonym for opportunity in the 21st-century economy. From artificial intelligence on the rise to the explosion of automation, digital developments mark a new turn in industries, workflows, and job requirements alike. Beneath these headlines dominated by technology, however, another quieter, yet no less significant, shift is occurring. Nontechnical careers are those in health, education, logistics, and public services, among others; these keep developing and expanding but also create rich opportunities for people who may never fit the mold of a 'tech' worker or perhaps simply like to contribute to different fashions. Far from becoming obsolete or under threat, these fields of career still form part of an essential subset of a well-rounded and resilient workforce, further being the bedrock of society's future.

Trends In The Global Workforce - Technology Redefines But Does Not Replace Jobs

As automation and artificial intelligence rapidly expand, an end is envisioned for any current human activity. Reality is a bit more nuanced. Though technology surely touches every profession, it does not take the place of workers. Instead, it changes the nature of work and often increases demand for jobs that complement, rather than substitute for, technology. The skills of customer service representatives, logistics coordinators, healthcare professionals, and many others have become more valuable in a world that depends on a balance between technological and human capabilities.

In a technology-driven economy, adaptability is an essential ingredient. A great deal of nontechnical work requires people to be basic users of digital tools, but the heart of the work remains in skills that are pretty hard for machines to replace: emotional intelligence, problem-solving, creative thinking, and effective communication. For example, though AI will help doctors make diagnoses, it doesn't substitute for the empathy and concern a healthcare professional offers. It goes further to the education industry where online learning aids facilitate the transfer of knowledge but cannot replace the mentorship and guidance of a well-trained teacher.

The Resilience Of Non-Tech Careers - Why These Jobs Matter More Than Ever

But these non-technical jobs have permanence, and durability in fact, just because they relate to the basic needs of humans and to the functional structure of society. For example, health care will continue to provide scope for competent practitioners who can look after the aging population. Education still requires teachers who can inspire, challenge, and mentor students. As urban centers begin to grow, skilled trades including electricians, carpenters, and construction managers will be in even greater demand due to new city development projects and sustainable infrastructure initiatives across the globe.

With the growth of the technology industry comes economic growth and the "ripple effects" on other industries that require non-technology-related jobs. Where the growth of the tech industry goes, so too do the increasing demands for HR professionals, project managers, and compliance officers who keep these companies running smoothly. So are logistics and supply chain professionals, fundamental to delivering products around the world, and marketing and communications roles, core drivers of brand visibility and engagement.

Emerging Roles And The Non-Visible Job Market

Industry lines become more muddled, and new roles emerge from this. Product innovation cuts across industries, and "industry convergence" alters traditional jobs, developing entirely new categories of work. Healthcare and wellness tourism blend into each other to open their respective grounds for professionals who understand both areas of medical care and hospitality. Education is integrating with corporate training, and curriculum designers and vocational trainers need to acquire skills in both pedagogy and specific professional sectors. Environmental services form a new expanding sector that includes sustainable agriculture, eco-friendly supply chains, and green construction practices.

The geographic distribution of these roles is also shifting, with emergent job clusters in sustainable city initiatives, health innovation hubs, and education innovation hotspots. Understanding the location of these emerging job clusters- urban areas of developed nations, but also growing urban hotspots in emerging markets-provides many workers with a good vantage point in situating themselves for future careers. Future-Proof Career Principles: Strategies for Long-Term Success

Professionals must adopt some principles that would guide them through growth and changes in careers over time in order to work prosperously amidst this change. A central principle of such an approach is the "multi-modal career," which involves the building of skills across a number of domains for a fluid transition between roles and industries as market demands shift. For example, a person who begins by working in logistics may later apply those organizing skills within healthcare administration, which similarly prizes the same sets of skills.

Another key principle is understanding "industry convergence"—the way a range of industries coalesce into new ones. As jobs continue to shift, the workers who are able to recognize and adapt to industry convergence will find themselves much better positioned to attain jobs within fields that are emerging. For example, the demand for brands to narrate stories in healthcare is on the rise, especially within an industry where practice will increasingly shift towards patient engagement. As one can pick each of these initial indications of an industry shift and convert them into up-skilling opportunities, one can better be ahead of a future set of demands.

Why This Book Matters - Career Adaptability And Lifelong Learning

It should serve as a guide for the young professional, the newly graduated, and those repositioning themselves in the changing job market. For the young professional, it gives direction as to where industries may provide stability and development. For the mid-career professional, it is a call that even with technological changes around them, they too can adapt and find some new sense of purpose. And for fresh grads who might feel intimidated by the rising tide of technology jobs, this book provides a comforting review of how many career options still exist beyond coding and software development.

A Fresh New Way To Show Off Careers Off The Beaten Track Of Technology.

Much has been said about what the future of work will look like amidst rapid technological change and automation but rarely is much attention given to those fields where no such interventions will take center stage. This book shines a spotlight on all of the non-tech fields that will drive job creation and economic resilience going forward. Healthcare and environmental services, public sector jobs, skilled trades-from solar and wind to electrical and plumbing and so many other jobs are not only viable but crucial to creating a balanced and inclusive workforce to meet the diversified needs of society. The approach to this book has relied heavily on analysis and predictions based on existing industry data and trends. It will detail industry segments that are going to witness significant job growth using metrics such as resistance to automation and demand for specialized human skills. Studying this metric data provides the reader with a data-driven vision of where non-tech job opportunities are going to likely thrive well into the next decade.

Methodology And Research Approach

This book is based on a comprehensive research effort that takes into consideration some of the key metrics in finding which sectors and roles offer the most significant potential for robust job growth and stability. Key factors include jobs that are resilient to shocks, have the potential for industry growth, and the evolving skill demands that accompany these trends. Diversified by a focus on resilience to automation, each industry profiled here has been selected with an ability to offer meaningful, sustainable employment options for individuals who may prefer roles centered around human interaction, creativity, and problem-solving.

The analysis of the book also considers the geographic trend, in which some industries will emerge in developed countries while others will emerge in emerging regions. This geographic mapping of opportunity enables readers to view things on a global scale, where they can look for emerging jobs and align their career aspirations with broader trends within the workforce.

Embracing Change And Building A Balanced Workforce

The future of non-technical careers is bright amidst a world that's increasingly technology-based. Even though technology will continue to affect the nature of industries and how we go about working, the need for non-technical jobs in the economic and human mechanisms will remain necessary. An unusual combination found in these jobs, such as empathy and communication, problem-solving, and adaptability, makes such a career vital even as the world continues to go digital.

In this new landscape, people need to be adaptive, learn, and be willing to change. This book will be your tool, insight, and strategy for building a career that at the same time is future-proof and personally fulfilling. This offers a pathway to success in industries that are not traditionally recognized to be technological but are just as important to forging the future. Through a thorough explanation of these fields, readers will understand in detail where the opportunities lie—and how to seize them.

CHAPTER 2: HEALTHCARE AND WELLNESS

The Expanding Scope Of Non-Tech Jobs

In a world where technology reshapes industries with breakneck speed, healthcare, and wellness have emerged as sectors impacted by technology, yet fundamentally human-centered. The needs arising from an aging population, changing lifestyle preferences, and improved awareness of mental health issues in the world increase the demands for non-technical roles in healthcare quickly and continuously. Unlike many industries, automation does not easily take over health and wellness because it relies on empathy, people skills, and an intuitive understanding of human well-being outside the scope of technology. This chapter will explore both traditional and changing professions in these areas, and detail the opportunities open to those who have chosen to work in these human-centered professions.

Aging Populations And Increased Care Needs

Demographically, populations around the world are aging. With increased life expectancy, various forms of care are necessary in order to enable the elderly to overcome the complex conditions and complications of old age. Implications are consequently huge: from a larger need for home healthcare workers to expanded requirements for physical therapists, occupational therapists, and other specialists geriatric professionals. With that, the World Health Organization projects that by 2050, more than two billion people will be aged 60 and above. Certainly, it calls for scalability in care systems backed by compassion. In response, health systems across continents are redesigning, and various roles are emanating with specific needs in elderly care. The home caregivers and community health aides are indispensable, as they provide in-house support to let the elderly live independently with professional assistance. To that end, it would require practitioners who are skilled in delivering medical support, as well as communicating effectively and managing complex health needs within a domestic setting. In addition, given the growing importance of physical therapists in the clinical management of aging populations to ensure mobility, autonomy, and quality of life, this is also a relatively promising career with vast opportunities for growth.

Preventative And Holistic Health - A New Paradigm For Wellness

As people increasingly put their well-being at the top of their priorities, the whole landscape of health has also expanded to preventive and holistic health services. The concept of wellness expanded to include physical fitness, nutrition, mental health, and even financial wellness. Hence, various careers in wellness coaching, nutrition counseling, and mental health advocacy likewise sprouted. Wellness coaches help their clients develop an individualized health plan that typically includes mindfulness practices, exercises, and nutritionally balanced diets, which can help prevent ailments and lead a better quality of life. Nutritionists and dietitians, too, are in great demand in this preventative approach by helping customers attain health goals by making diet adjustments that will help with long-term health outcomes. Their expertise in managing and reducing risk factors through diet has made them highly valuable in an age where chronic diseases, such as diabetes and cardiovascular disease, are on the rise. Mental health was once stigmatized and left unattended; however, it is now recognized for playing a very important role in total wellness. This development has raised the demand for mental health counselors, therapists, and clinical psychologists who are well-equipped to deal with stress, anxiety, and more. With greater awareness of mental health, the reach of professional work for resilience and emotional wellness extends further into individuals and communities.

Specialty Roles And Emergent Sub-Industries

Within health care and wellness, a number of specialty roles and sub-industries are at an emergent stage, offering opportunities for professionals with focused expertise in the above-mentioned areas. Cost, regulatory, and resource efficiency factors are increasingly playing a larger role in managing healthcare, making the area even more complex for organizations. With skilled healthcare administrators in demand, one can expect management responsibilities in strategic planning to staff management in hospitals, clinics, and long-term care facilities. Public health policy is another fertile ground that offers career growth to individuals, especially those who want to contribute to shaping health programs and policies that would affect communities from a larger perspective.

The healthcare industry has now merged with other growing industries in providing services to offer tourism-related wellness, which involves travel experiences centered on improving an individual's health and relaxing. This ranges from spa retreats that focus on mental health to wellness resorts that cater to physical health through exercise and nutrition. Similarly, recreational health industries have made their niches by targeting health-conscious individuals who want to fulfill their health goals by taking part in lifestyle activities like hiking, meditation, and exercise tourism. All these cross-industry careers will integrate healthcare hospitality and recreation in a host of career opportunities in holistic health services.

Unique Insights - Convergence Of Health And Tourism, Wellness Tourism, And Recreational Health

As lifestyles become more health-oriented, the boundaries between healthcare and leisure industries begin to blur. Wellness tourism is that aspect of tourism that incorporates healthcare into travel and includes experiences for the rejuvenation of the mind and body. Wellness tourism serves a wide range of demographics-from the de-stressing of young professionals to retirees wanting proactive health management. For healthcare professionals, this means a unique but satisfying career path marrying clinical knowledge with customer service and hospitality skills.

Another interesting aspect of this industry is recreational health, including those with outdoor fitness, adventure sports, and spa wellness. Such services allow job opportunities in special settings and comprise eco-resorts as well as the large hub of urban wellness centers targeted at clients who want to combine health goals with a lifestyle. Some of such professionals are wellness coordinators, recreational health advisors, and lifestyle coaches who divert focus toward preventive care through lifestyle and not medical intervention. The rise of this industry only confirms a huge cultural shift: health and wellness can no longer remain peripheral to life; they are about practices that demand continuous participation by individuals.

The Growing Use Of Technology In Health And Wellness

While healthcare and wellness are distinctly human-centric, technology allows furtherance into the future of these industries. Digital health tools, wearables, and telehealth have transformed access to healthcare, particularly in remote and underserved areas. Today, caregivers are working in environments that have incorporated data-driven insights, enhancing the care of patients through a journey of wearable technology worn to continuously track vital signs and into virtual counseling for mental health via telehealth platforms.

These technological changes also reach managerial positions, whose work is smoothed by data analysis and patient management software. However, these features have not nullified the need for individuals in the manual function areas; instead, they have emphasized the significance of human knowledge as all these advanced technologies are accompanied by the incorporation of individuals who interpret the same digital information within a personal encounter. A healthcare professional now is also to include an interpretation of the digital information into a personal encounter that helps foster trust and clarity between the patients and their providers.

A Future With Abundant Non-Technical Jobs:

A bright future in health and wellness, wherein growth, diversity, and adaptability are words that may sum it up, awaits. While the sector is sure to be one brimming with opportunities for hands-on work in patient care to wellness coaching and across to healthcare management still can retain the human touch and compassion even in the face of increased efficiency and access availed by digital tools.

For those in search of a professional trail that can balance resilience with purpose, healthcare, and wellness promise stability besides the reward of touching other people's lives directly. As populations age and preventive and holistic health solutions see increasing demand, it follows that practitioners are going to become all the more pivotal to societal well-being by meeting needs that are as basic as they are enduring. In these times, when industries are shaped by technology, health care and wellness stand as refreshing indications that some of the most valuable work depends not on automation, but on those irreplaceable qualities: human connection and care.

It is within this landscape that both healthcare and wellness professionals play a major role not only within traditional auspices but also in emergent domains reflecting inchoate social values with regard to health and quality of life. This chapter serves as an entry into exploring these career paths where the future for non-technical jobs could not have been so fulfilling, and secure, and an opportunity to make a very meaningful difference in other people's lives.

CHAPTER 3: EDUCATION AND TRAINING

Reinventing Learning For The Future

The landscape of education and training is changing; traditional models are having to adapt to the changing landscape of workforce needs. In a period when automation, digital transformation, and other industry-specific developments are shaping job markets, continuous lifelong learning has become ever more necessary. Professions develop new dimensions outside formal education that have to be harnessed through rising corporate training, adult education, and skills development programs.

For this reason, lifelong learning has become a corporate cultural cliché of emphasis on the enhancement of skills regularly. Unlike the days when education was left to the early years of life, upskilling and reskilling are becoming an element of the modern workforce through most career cycles. Today, workers want knowledge that stands the test of time, thus enabling them to make contributions that prevail in industry needs compelled to renew with trends and technologies. Organizations that adopt this form of education can easily take turns on their industries due to change, providing a labor force able to engage present needs and even move up the ladder to meet challenges.

Growing Need For Lifelong Learning

The urge to pursue lifelong learning stems from the fact that the traditional trends of education can no longer help with the rapidly changing needs that are witnessed today in various careers. Specialized knowledge in areas of health care, green energy, logistics, and even digital literacy is now needed as a must for people to get by. It has, therefore, emerged as a high-growth sector, facilitating the learning of professionals in the comfort of their workplace. Large companies are acting positively in investing in educational resources for their employees, realizing that only skillful adaptation can ensure business success.

The move is further propelled by the change in expectations of the new generation of employees. Millennial and Gen Z employees look more at personal development and career growth; hence, they like an employer that offers a wide array of learning opportunities. Companies, in turn, have come up with opportunities for learning so that there will be diversified skills, especially in fields such as management, technical proficiency, and soft skills. Such opportunities are proposed with the intent of enabling employees to grow into different roles, thus building an adaptable and resilient workforce that fits within the organizational goals.

Increasingly Diverse Roles In Education And Training

With the emphasis on lifelong learning, new professional profiles are emerging in education. Curriculum designers now create focused training modules, tailor-made to the needs of the industry, while education consultants offer their services to assist companies in implementing proper learning strategies for the corporate environment. This specialist knows the particularities of adult learning and thus tries many approaches-from traditional formats in the classroom to virtual and hybrid models-to make educational offerings effective and accessible.

Moreover, with the increasing demand for digitally literate trainers, there arises a corresponding need to make staff members aware of the usage of digital platforms and tools. These would train and guide such employees on how to attain maximum productivity and competitiveness within a technically evolving environment. This is evident in various fields where this is highly essential, such as finance, health, and logistics.

It isn't that roles in education exist only within large organizations. Startups and smaller companies also invest in training to develop their teams, albeit on a more modest scale. Most use specialized consultants who design the training programs or facilitate workshops; this is how smaller organizations can be competitive without stretching resources too far. This reflects the democratization of professional learning, ensuring access across varied structures of organizations.

Specialized Vocational Training: A Growth Sector

Specialized vocational training is gaining importance as industries realize that they require a focused set of skills and knowledge in areas like green energy, healthcare, and skilled trades. Since the concept of economies is drifting towards 'greener' ideas, certain sets of professions related to renewable energy sectors involve specialization that is not provided through conventional systems of education. Similarly, requirements in the field of health care range from higher levels of patient care to medical technology, necessitating vocational courses tailored to meet the demands of specific sectors.

For these reasons, vocational training is evolving to meet these demands for such an education through highly specialized, yet less time-consuming programs. Such vocational classes pertaining to renewable energy would include solar installation, biofuel management, and wind energy maintenance. This kind of structure allows for an increasingly focused and intense way into lucrative and in-demand professions. The same thing holds true with health care, from training programs for medical technicians, through health administrators to home caregivers, in order to guarantee a continuous supply of skills in an ageing world population.

This covers even the so-called 'unnoticed industries' that form part of the logistics, construction, and food services, the latter two of which are indispensable to life. Because these industries still do provide room for stable employment, they require updated knowledge now due to their continuously changing technologies and industry standards. This goes without saying that in proportion to how these industries continue their course of expansion, vocational education will remain constantly indispensable in preparing the workers capable of these specialized jobs.

Unique Insights: Synergies And Partnerships Shaping The Future Of Education

One of the unique developments in education is the increasing synergy between online education, vocational training, and corporate partnerships. Online platforms thus provide flexibility and access to the acquisition of skills and credentials, while corporate collaborations add depth of insight into specific industry needs. Such partnership of education providers and corporations, through aligning content with practical requirements, helps learners develop relevant in-demand skills.

This model takes on a partnership-driven approach, with benefits for both the learner and the employer. Students develop skills useful for practical application, increasing employability, while companies have the advantage of an already skilled workforce. Indeed, many corporations are already working with online platforms to co-develop courses in digital marketing, project management, or data analysis. In such courses, companies can invest in the creation of talent without having to take the effort and time in-house to train them over many years, thus reducing costs and getting a ready workforce immediately.

The inextricable linking of education with a career path gives a whole new meaning to lifelong learning. Innovation happens at a pace where even a professional well into his or her career still needs to be in the learning mode. A future where education extends beyond the traditional setting opens opportunities and career growth paths that further support continuous professional development.

The Global Shift In Learning - Embracing An Education-Centric Workforce

There is fast-growing awareness in the contemporary world that economic stability to a great extent depends upon a resilient and adaptable workforce.

In countries where an aging population is being experienced, such as Japan and several European nations, education takes center stage to compensate for their shrinking labor pools. These countries encourage older workers to prolong their employed lives through continuous education and enhancement of skills necessary for the evolving requirements of industry.

As such, rapidly growing economies put more emphasis on equipping their younger populations with the right competencies in sectors that spur economic growth. In this respect, countries in Southeast Asia tend to further encourage technical education in manufacturing, IT services, and renewable energies.

The rising trend consequently epitomizes two approaches to education-one for mature markets and the other for emerging economies through targeted strategies.

Education and training now offer a whole new exciting field of prospects for professionals: growth in education consultants, curriculum designers, and vocational trainers is likely to increase as demand for lifelong learning and education in specific skills continues. Whether as a career path or a stepping stone within other industries, education, and training are the fields that will provide professionals with an avenue to create tangible impacts while keeping careers relevant in an ever-changing world.

Education and training will continue to develop in the direction of what the mixed energetic workforce of today needs. With the growth of new jobs and specialized training curricula, the industry will be at the cutting edge in preparing people for the future, emphasizing again and again lifelong learning and flexibility. This chapter underlines the significant position education holds within the evolving non-technical professions landscape and sets it at the heart of economic strength and individual well-being.

CHAPTER 4: ENVIRONMENTAL SERVICES AND SUSTAINABILITY

Careers Of A Green Economy

The emergence of sustainable practices in different sectors, as the world strives to find urgently needed solutions for pressingly challenging environmental problems, has therefore opened vast career opportunities in a green economy. A climate-friendly, resource-efficient, responsible management, and ecological restoration- creating an emerging demand by governments, corporations, and consumers. This now births a full-fledged sector on environmental services and sustainability, hence offering careers that tend to urgent global needs while contributing towards a more sustainable future.

The rise in careers in environmental services marks a deep shift in how industries are working. Sustainability is no longer peripheral or niche but core to business strategies across sectors. Companies are also investing in sustainable practices, from agriculture and energy to construction and consumer goods, as an ethical imperative and long-term economic strategy. The chapter discusses how the green economy opens up non-technical jobs in sustainable development fields like climate policy compliance, renewable energy, and supply chain management.

The Impact Of Global Climate Policies On Job Creation

International policy changes to deal with climate change have thus promoted far-reaching changes in job markets. The Paris Agreement, the European Green Deal, and national targets for reduction of emissions increase demand for professionals skilled both in regulatory compliance and environmental management. In such contexts, new job roles that have emerged include those comprising a climate policy analyst, an environmental consultant, and a sustainability officer - these shall be the professionals who will be able to bridge the gap between what regulatory requirements are and how they can be implemented within an organization.

For example, environmental compliance officers liaise with different companies in bringing their activities to the requested national and international levels of emissions, waste management, and energy efficiency. These positions are especially highly relevant to the manufacturing, agricultural, and transport industries, where the environmental effects are really large. In brief, as fresh policies emerge, professionals who know in-depth about regulatory frameworks and sustainable practices will be significantly required by companies as they try to align their operations with global environmental objectives.

The themes that keep emerging in this area include considerations of the "circular economy" in which business operations make every effort to eliminate waste and fully utilize resources. This, in turn, has created jobs that can be conceptualized in terms of closed-loop supply chains, waste minimization, and sustainable manufacturing. As more and more industries start embracing the circular economic model, jobs will be created around waste management strategies, sustainable sourcing, and product lifecycle analysis.

Renewable Energy Infrastructure Is Fast Emerging As A Source Of Employment.

One of the most significant growth areas in environmental services is certainly renewable energy. As various countries move away from a fossil fuel-based economy, there has been an explosion not only in clean energy sources such as wind, solar, and biofuels but also in non-technical jobs associated with those industries. This sector has a wide range of roles that span from project management and policy advocacy to logistics, hence becoming fertile ground for professionals in sustainability.

In renewable energy, project coordinators, energy analysts, and community engagement specialists have become highly relevant. Especially project coordinators have borne major responsibilities for the construction and management of renewable energy infrastructures, ensuring that projects operate within budget and in accordance with local environmental standards. Such jobs more often than not require a mix of organizational ability and environmental awareness, as the project coordinators will have to navigate through complex regulatory environments and stakeholder interests.

Renewable energy-related community involvement roles also reveal the social aspect of the green economy. As an example, outreach specialists for the community aim to increase the knowledge level and awareness of the community about renewable projects by means of decreasing concerns and increasing support for projects that are sustainable. Communication is of great significance in such jobs since it includes explaining the economic and environmental benefits of renewable energy to a wide range of stakeholders.

On the other hand, energy analysts are crucial in the analysis of environmental and economic viability regarding projects that install renewable energy. They study data to determine optimal installation sites, forecast returns that might be expected, and assess various sources of energy for sustainability. These roles give essential insight into the effective large-scale adoption of clean energy with the growing infrastructure of renewable energy.

Sustainable Consumer Products And The Rise Of Green Supply Chains

It has therefore increased the demand for professionals who have the skills for eco-friendly consumer product supply chain management and ethical sourcing. Firms are revising their supply chains to reduce environmental impact and increase transparency as more consumers become environmentally conscious. The concern for supply chain management careers involves assurance that products are sourced, manufactured, and delivered with minimal environmental harm and social responsibility in mind.

Specialists ensure that the materials used during production are eco-friendly, that suppliers promote fair labor practices, and that methods of transportation curb carbon emissions. A sustainable sourcing manager working for a global retailer may be tasked with finding suppliers utilizing recyclable materials, further reducing the ecological footprint of a company, while answering the need for an increase in consumers who demand 'green' products.

The influence of sustainability does not stay with sourcing only but also with product design and packaging. Sustainable product design jobs aim at the discovery of products with minimal resources utilized and almost none waste generated. These employees work in tandem with product development teams to ensure that recyclable or biodegradable materials are used in the making of a product or ensure that the design can be modified to meet emerging environmental standards. Packaging being one of the bigger contributors to waste is another area primed for innovation. There are highly sought-after job roles in the field of sustainable packaging, whereby companies look to reduce plastic use and improve recyclability to make their products more attractive to grow raft of environmentally-conscious consumers.

Government-Backed Sustainability Programs As Catalysts For Careers

The government initiatives also cannot be underplayed in driving careers in sustainability. Most governments have instituted ways of encouraging companies to go green, either through funding or tax credits, among other forms of resources that spur business operations with little harmful effect on the environment. This support creates a steady demand for professionals who can develop, manage, and monitor these government-backed programs in sustainability.

For instance, green building-related initiatives in the U.S. have paved the way for careers like that of energy auditors and/or building certification specialists whose responsibility is to assess properties for energy efficiency. Various similar career routes are equally available in the European Union, which mandates environmental assessments as part of compliance with the EU's strict environmental policies. This ensures that both public and private sector buildings are energy efficient while the government works toward its emissions-cutting goals and urban sustainability.

Other government-backed roles involve outreach and education of the public for involvement in sustainability matters. Environmental educators, policy advocates, and outreach coordinators help local governments advance sustainable practices and give the community information about climate action initiatives. These are important positions for marshaling public support for sustainability programs and leading communities toward greener practices.

The Intersection Of Profit And Purpose In Sustainability Careers

With the environment turning into a competitive differentiator, companies embracing sustainability secure their place for a long period. Sustainability professionals enable organizations not only to minimize their ecological footprint but also to improve brand reputation, meeting consumer expectations regarding corporate responsibility. That sweet spot where purpose and profit merge seems to be attracting a new generation of professionals who are passionate about impact through their work.

In the case of careers outside of the technical realm that carry meaning for the professional, environmental services and sustainability present opportunities to make a difference in areas critical to the future of the planet. Careers can be anything from compliance with global policies on climate to the advancement of green energy projects and the driving of sustainable consumer practices they can influence in a myriad of ways. With the growth of the green economy, a path to meaningful employment is created one that is in keeping with social responsibility and also one that shows care for the environment and thus will create the bedrock for sustainable development in all sectors.

The future of non-technical careers, therefore, meets the sustainability platform in as far as environmental awareness should permeate all functions within business operations. Indeed, professionals not only contribute to global climate goals with such roles but also help forge a workforce that is resilient and driven by purpose. In so many ways, the green economy is not only an emerging economic opportunity but also a movement toward a sustainable world, offering jobs combining strategic insight, industry innovation, and the mission of building a more sustainable planet.

CHAPTER 5: HOSPITALITY, TRAVEL, AND TOURISM

New Services Of Same Industries

That is the shape the global hospitality, travel, and tourism sector has taken: a metamorphosis influenced by altered consumer choices, technology advancement, and an increased desire for sustainable practice. From this unprecedented disruption of the global pandemic, this resilient industry emerges rather than merely recovering-into reinventing for the demands of today's traveler. It creates innumerable opportunities for non-tech-savvy professionals.

The Renaissance Of Global Travel

This is the post-pandemic period, which industry players term the "revenge travel" phenomenon, where pent-up demand catalyzes a robust recovery in global tourism. However, this resurgence bears a dramatically different look from the pre-pandemic patterns. Today, travelers are in pursuit of more meaningful and authentic experiences; thus, opportunities have been created for professionals capable of crafting and delivering such distinctive journeys.

This transition has led to many other specialized jobs within the industry: experience designers create immersive cultural programs other than sightseeing; local cultural liaisons bridge the visitors and communities: and sustainability coordinators make sure tourism practices match environmental conservation objectives. These are jobs that require people who have strong interpersonal skills, cultural sensitivity, and a sense of sustainable practices enough to fend off automated technology and other artificial replacements.

The Changing World Of Hospitality Services

In the hospitality industry, the concept of standardized service provisions has shifted to developing personalized experiences. These days, it is not about offering five-star facilities in the hotel but rather moments and stories. The new jobs invented are proof of that, like guest experience managers, wellness concierges, and cultural programming directors.

The personalized and lifestyle hotels have begun to become major drivers of growth, for which professionals with the ability to curate distinctive experiences of local character with adherence to international service standards are sought. These properties are looking for staff who would be able to act as local ambassadors, offering authentic insights and introductions to the culture, history, and community of their destination.

Emerging Niche Markets

The specialized market segments have equally seen phenomenal growth as a means of reaching markets oriented toward specific interests and values. What started as a niche, ecotourism has grown into a mainstream preference with travelers increasingly seeking experiences that have a minimum environmental impact while offering the maximum positive contributions to host communities. Events of this nature drive up demand for specialists in sustainable tourism operations, assessment of environmental impacts, and management of community relations.

Another big growth area is that of adventure tourism and "glamping." These call for professionals who can marry outdoor expertise with a more luxury level of service: from adventure guides who have safety certification to hospitality managers capable of maintaining five-star standards in the most secluded locations. Wellness tourism has expanded beyond spa services to holistic health, which involves designing wellness programs, nutritionists, and mind-body practitioners.

Technology-Enhanced Human Service On The Rise

Though technology is playing an increasingly pivotal role in travel and hospitality, it ironically has increased the humanness of the industry. Computers may handle reservations and simple questions, but that has just increased the resonance of meaningful human contacts in service provision. Today, hospitality professionals are challenged to do what technology alone cannot: providing the personal touch.

There are new positions created to bridge the gap between people and technology. An experienced technology coordinator ensures that digital conveniences heighten the personal service without removing it. Virtual concierges merge digital efficiency with human friendliness to make sure day-to-day support is available round the clock. These are positions needing professionals who understand technology but are great with people.

Training And Development In The Contemporary Hospitality Industry

With the growth and changing face of hospitality services, there has been a greater demand for professionals in training and development. Such professionals are engaged in designing and delivering appropriate programs aimed at assisting the staff to deliver excellence in service, along with accepting new technology and fulfilling guests' expectations. The industry especially needs trainers who can train teams on emotional intelligence, cultural awareness, and customized service delivery.

Evolution Of Events And MICE Sector

With time, some segments of the MICE industry have evolved and opened up new avenues for event professionals. Hybrid event planners create events that will integrate live and online elements smoothly. Sustainability event managers plan large events that are specifically aimed at achieving environmental thresholds without compromising the quality of the experience.

Career Paths And Skill-Sets

Success in modern hospitality depends on the combination of timeless and new skills: while the essentials of guest service are still important, the professional must develop the following, among others :

- Cultural Intelligence - to work effectively across cultural boundaries and create inclusive experiences for a diverse range of guests
- Sustainability Competencies - knowledge of environmental best practices and applying eco-friendly initiatives
- Experience Design - creating memorable, personalized experiences through communicating brand values
- Crisis Management: How one deals with situations arising unexpectedly but still offers a quality service.
- Digital Literacy: Comfort with technology, maintaining humanness in interaction.

Future Outlook And Opportunities

The hospitality, travel, and tourism industries are ever-changing; a range of trends will continue to shape future opportunities, including:

- The growth in personalized and authentic experiences will create opportunities for specialists who can design special guest pathways.
- The emphasis on sustainability will see continued growth in demand for professionals who can implement and manage environmentally friendly operations.
- Increased attention to health and transformational tourism would open a wide horizon to specialists in health, wellness, and personal development.
- High-end adventure tourism became increasingly popular, increasing demand for those professionals who can offer a high-end service in unique locations

Chapter Brief

Hospitality, travel, and tourism remain some of the fastest-growing industries providing several different career options that are not technical. Technology might change the phase of this industry, but the roots or the emphatic, creative, and personal connective elements of hospitality cannot be emulated by complete automation. Along with knowing current traveler trends and modern sustainability practices, those core competencies will bring a professional to many satisfying careers.

Only those professionals will thrive in this constant process who are able to make necessary adjustments to their methods and practices according to the constantly changing situation in the market. The future of hospitality lies not in replacing the human touch with technology but in enabling meaningful connections, and the facilitation of memorable experiences which a technological alternative alone is incapable of providing.

CHAPTER 6: SKILLED TRADES AND MANUFACTURING

A New Era For Blue-Collar Jobs

Skilled trades and manufacturing are at the cusp of a transformative era that forces new perceptions onto this job market while creating unrivaled opportunities for career advancement. It is a kind of renaissance in the work category commonly referred to as 'blue-collar' labor so spurred on by the integrating technology, imperatives of sustainability, and the appreciating awareness of the integral position such professions hold within the modern economy.

Modern Renaissance Of Skilled Trades

The skilled trades are in what many industry experts would refer to as a "Golden Age of Opportunity." From aging infrastructure renovation to new construction booms across both developed and emerging markets, skilled tradespeople are in higher demand than ever. Electricians, plumbers, welders, and HVAC technicians are no longer just maintenance workers; they're becoming highly skilled professionals who marry traditional craftsmanship with modern technical knowledge.

This change is nowhere better embodied than in the changing nature of electrical trades. Today, electricians need to know not just traditional wiring but also smart home systems, the integration of renewable energy, and industrial automation. Similarly, today's HVAC technicians work with sophisticated climate control systems that require knowledge in both mechanical systems and digital controls.

Domestic Manufacturing Revival

A dramatic change is underway in the global manufacturing landscape, with companies increasingly seeking to re-shore and nearshore. Supply chain vulnerabilities highlighted by recent global disruptions accelerated this trend, causing a renaissance in domestic manufacturing across the developed world. But these new manufacturing operations bear little resemblance to the factories of the past.

The modern factory is filled with a skilled workforce operating sophisticated equipment, with knowledge of quality control procedures, and making rapid changes in the method of production. The precision machinist, quality assurance specialist, and production team leader have joined electricians, plumbers, and other skilled trades in the application of new technologies to augment rather than replace the human dimension of skill and judgment.

The Sustainability Revolution In Trades

Environmentalism has become a driving force in the continuing development of the skilled trades. The increasing focus on sustainable construction and energy efficiency brings specialized positions that did not exist just ten years ago. Solar installation technicians, green building specialists, and energy efficiency auditors are part of this new breed of skilled workers who merge classic trade skills with environmental know-how.

Likewise, sustainability has given birth to new occupations within the manufacturing industry as companies seek professionals who can apply and maintain green production processes. For this reason, sustainable materials specialists, manufacturing process waste reduction specialists, and energy efficiency specialists in manufacturing processes are in high demand as companies comply with environmental legislation and meet consumer demand for greener products.

Advanced Materials And Special Skills

Such new materials and building techniques have created niches for specialists able to work with advanced composites, prefabricated components, and sustainable materials. Such newly emerging roles require professionals versed in traditional craftsmanship and modern materials science. In this regard, composite material technicians apply traditional fabrication skills to their knowledge of advanced materials properties.

Manufacturing today requires a large and increasing array of specialists able to process everything from advanced, high-performance polymers to biodegradable composites. Many of these roles combine an unusual blend of hands-on competencies and technical knowledge, creating new career tracks that reach across traditional manufacturing and materials science.

The Function Of Trade Schools And Professional Development

Skilled trades have evolved to such a degree that now, more than ever, the demand for specialized education and continuous professional development is highly important. Modern trade schools are now reformed into complex, technical institutes that combine practical, hands-on training with higher technological education. Many institutions of these kinds collaborate with industry leaders to guarantee that their curricula remain current in comparison with the actual market requirements.

Professional certification programs also mirror the increasing sophistication in the modern trades, providing specialized credentials that vouch for those facts. This often means that classical skills assessment is combined with training on new technologies and sustainable practices to provide unambiguous career routes for skilled professionals.

Integrating Digital Skills

While skilled trades have been and always will be hands-on professions, for many, increasing digital literacy has become important. Digital tools today provide the foundation for many modern tradespersons as they plan projects and diagnose systems. BIM technology has joined the requisite toolbox of many construction trades as professionals marry physical skills with digital competency.

The integration of digital systems in manufacturing has, on one hand, brought with it the requirement for a professional who can marry conventional production processes with digital control systems. Such hybrid jobs require people comfortable with both physical manufacturing processes and digital interfaces.

Future Prospects And Career Paths

Skilled trades and manufacturing offer a number of career-building avenues. Most progress from a few occupations into supervisory roles, but some specialize in emerging areas like renewable energy systems or advanced manufacturing processes. Greater sophistication in these sectors has also led to many opportunities for skilled professionals to move into training, consulting, or business ownership.

Global Opportunities And Standards

This standardization has internationalized not only construction and manufacturing but also given skilled professionals opportunities to work anywhere, in any part of the world. Most of these trades have international standards of certification, and as such, they are portable across borders. Global standardization has opened up enormous opportunities for specialists in the related fields of industrial maintenance, precision manufacturing, and sustainable construction.

Chapter Brief

The transformation of the skilled trades and manufacturing sector presents a great opportunity to all those individuals seeking rewarding and stable careers outside the traditional office environments. These sectors give satisfaction in terms of tangible accomplishments while providing opportunities to work with cutting-edge technologies and sustainable practices.

These skilled occupations open very promising career prospects with great growth potential to professionals who would be willing to amalgamate traditional skills with current technical knowledge. As these sectors continue to evolve, so, too, does the sophistication and reward for those individuals who value skilled craftsmanship in the modern economy.

CHAPTER 7: PUBLIC SECTOR AND NONPROFITS

Careers That Bring Purpose And Stability In A World Faced With Global Challenges And Social Transformation.

In these times, the public and nonprofit sectors have appeared as crucial change agents. Demographic shifts, environmental concerns, and a change in social dynamics set the pace for the great evolution of these sectors.

The Modern Public Sector - Beyond Traditional Government Roles

The public sector today little resembles what the popular imagination considers this segment to be-institutional bureaucracies. Today, federal, state, and local government agencies are changing to reflect complex issues such as climate change, public health crises, and other evolving problems. Such evolution has ensured demand from professionals to be able to navigate intricate policy landscapes and deliver pragmatic solutions to community needs.

Nowadays, urban planners design resilient and livable cities while working at the crossroads of sustainability, technology, and community development. Public health officials coordinate sophisticated response systems through which responses against emerging health threats are devised, while environmental protection specialists build and implement policies that balance economic growth with ecological preservation.

This has brought with it a whole slew of new, unfamiliar titles that have cropped up within the past decade in the public sector. Climate resilience officers develop strategies to protect communities from environmental vulnerabilities. Digital service managers work on access and efficiencies related to government platforms. Community engagement specialists act as the bridge between agencies and diverse populations, making sure the voices of all citizens are reflected in public service.

Nonprofit Evolution - From Charity To Systemic Change

It has evolved from being a 'sector' marked by traditional charitable organizations to one featuring sophisticated entities willing to engage in systemic social change. Contemporary nonprofits practice business methodology and innovative strategies in trying to confront complex social concerns; thus opening the door for professionals across diverse skill spectrums.

Specialized social impact measurement specialists help organizations quantify their effectiveness and package impact communication. Development directors bring together traditional fundraising competencies with the skills of digital marketing to engage donors across multiple platforms. Program designers develop solutions that are scalable across multiple communities and contexts.

This growth is perhaps best exemplified by international NGOs that operate involved programs around the world and need professional managers who can handle cross-cultural contexts while maintaining consistent metrics of performance and impact. This would include program managers who oversee programs across many countries, cultural liaisons who can build relationships with local communities, and impact assessment specialists who can quantify program performance across diverse contexts.

The Emergence Of Mission-Driven Careers

The fact is that young professionals are increasingly drawn to mission-driven careers. This generation sees and identifies professional development with social impact, and public sector and nonprofit organizations are accepting modifications within their structures and cultures to help attract this type of talent.

Organizations nowadays provide sophisticated professional development programs, competitive benefit packages, and well-charted career progression routes. Many avail opportunities for global mobility-thus allowing professionals to gain international exposure to work for causes that are valuable to them. This evolution brought in the need for full-time talent development specialists who could develop such programs that balance mission focus with professional growth.

Keystone Skills And Competencies

Success in these sectors, therefore, requires a special blend of skills that combines traditional professional competencies with the requirements of modern challenges:

- Ability for strategic thinking and adaptability: Professionals have to know how to maneuver in complicated stakeholder environments while focusing on long-term goals. A policy analyst should understand immediate needs and the long-term implications of his or her recommendations.
- Cross-Sector Collaboration: One of the rapidly emerging competencies is the activity across boundaries among public, private, and nonprofit sectors. The partnership manager creates alliances to marshal needed resources and expertise from multiple sectors to achieve shared objectives.
- Financial Management: Modern public sector and nonprofit professionals are expected to understand complex financial instruments and funding mechanisms. As an example, grant managers must juggle increasingly complicated funding expectations with the sustainability imperatives of programs.
- Digital Literacy: These jobs aren't highly technical; rather, the professional needs to understand how to make the most of

technology in bringing social change. Digital transformation specialists help organizations leap into newer tools without losing sight of their key mission.

Upcoming Opportunities And Future Trends

Following are several trends that are acting to shape the future career opportunities in these sectors:

- Social Innovation: Due to the increased innovative solution development for social challenges, more and more job opportunities are opening their doors for professionals who can design and implement novel ways of looking at and working out problems that have plagued society for many years. Social innovation specialists mix business acumen with a deep understanding of social issues.
- Environmental Justice: The convergence of environmental and social justice issues has created new positions aimed at equitably distributing environmental benefits and burdens among all people. Environmental Justice Coordinators are involved in resolving the disproportionate environmental impacts of communities.
- Global Health Security: Emergent global health concerns have highlighted the necessity for practitioners who can help manage responses to health threats that cross borders. International Health Program Managers combine public health knowledge with cross-cultural communication skills.

The Future Of Purpose-Driven Work

The public sector and nonprofit organizations will continue to evolve with changing social needs and technological capabilities. The fundamental appeal, however, will remain the same to integrate professional development with significant social contribution.

It is the professionals who can keep the mission in focus as they adapt to new tools and approaches that will be successful in these fields. They have to balance a growing demand for efficiency and measurable results with the need to work towards addressing some of the most complex problems found in society, which will resist simple solutions.

Chapter Brief

The public sector and organizations within the nonprofit world offer valuable opportunities to people interested in careers that will bring stability with a sense of purpose. Both sectors continue to grow and provide challenging yet satisfying career opportunities for persons who would like to make their professional lives count by contributing to the social good.

Their future depends on the degree to which they would be able to attract and retain competent professionals who could successfully rise to such a complex challenge without losing sight of their mission and impact. Those steeling themselves to meld professional excellence with social purpose will find these sectors offering them a wealth of opportunities for meaningful, sustainable careers.

CHAPTER 8: REAL ESTATE AND URBAN DEVELOPMENT

Building Tomorrow's Communities

In the real estate and urban development landscape, the era of transformation seems at work in the integration of shifting demographics, imperatives for sustainability, and evolving lifestyles. As we journey further into the 21st century, the manner in which we design, construct, and manage living and working spaces presents unparalleled opportunities for those who are non-technical professionals right across the sector.

The Infrastructure Revolution

Globally, the infrastructure sector is in a state of renaissance underpinned by mega government investments complemented by initiatives in the private sector. The Infrastructure Investment and Jobs Act in the United States alone has committed over $1 trillion to rebuilding America's aged infrastructure, while similar initiatives are in place and unfolding across Europe and Asia. This is creating a surge in demand for infrastructure spending in construction managers, project coordinators, and site supervisors these roles place strong requirements on leadership and organizational competencies with less emphasis on technical expertise.

These infrastructure projects go beyond conventional transportation and utility networks. Modern infrastructure professionals are ever more engaged in smart city solutions, sustainable energy systems, and digital connectivity infrastructure development. While the technical experts may design such systems, it is the project managers and coordinators who oversee their successful realization, engage in the management of relationships with a variety of stakeholders, and assist the client in dealing with the complexities of regulatory environments.

Property Management Evolution

This property management sector has come a long way from its historical roots. Today, the property manager must face a manifold landscape of expectations from the tenant's perspective, demands regarding sustainability, and technological integrations. To date, with the development of more mixed-use projects and community-oriented living, a growing demand is arising for managers capable of creating dynamic, interesting environments appealing to residents and commercial tenants alike.

The massive work pattern shift that has happened since the global pandemic has really redefined what is expected of a property manager in commercial real estate today. Today, property managers are expected to have experience in managing flexible workspaces, the implementation of health and safety, and creating an environment that will support hybrid work models. As the ever-growing amenities and community-building continue to rise in today's commercial space, a new breed of "experience managers" has come forward who strive to make workplace environments engaging.

Sustainable Development And Green Building

Sustainability has changed from being a good-to-have feature to a basic necessity in the real estate development business. This change has provided so much scope for professionals to build expertise in sustainable building practices, environmental compliance, and green building certification. From LEED consultants to sustainability coordinators and environmental compliance managers, development teams today embrace such people as an integral part of the team, ensuring that projects meet the increasingly high standards in the environment.

Yet, the drive for sustainability now encompasses not just buildings but whole communities. New demands are made on the urban planner and developer to provide an environment that is user-friendly, has a minimal carbon footprint, and, wherever possible, green spaces. Growing demand is therefore placed on those professionals who are able to balance the sometimes-competing demands of environmental consideration, community needs, and economic viability.

Community-Led Urban Planning

The focus of modern urban development is increasingly community-based and social in impact. In that regard, urban planners and community development specialists are the pivotal professionals today in new developments responsive to diverse populations' needs while nurturing social cohesion. This has opened up opportunities for professionals with focus and acumen in stakeholder engagement, community outreach, and social impact assessment.

The so-called "placemaking" has come to the fore, enabling public spaces to help improve people's health, happiness, and well-being. Now, there is a need for professionals in Placemaking who will help develop urban spaces into active community hubs. They also have very diverse backgrounds in social sciences, arts, or community organizations and bring new insights into the process of urban development.

Affordable Housing And Social Impact

The global crisis over housing affordability has focused a lot of attention on the need for innovative strategies in affordable housing development. In its wake, it has created opportunities for those professionals who understand the complex junction of public policy and private development, along with the needs of the community. Jobs such as housing policy analyst, affordable housing developer, and community housing coordinator are growing in importance in the quest to address this vital social issue.

Social impact assessment and community benefits agreements have long been some of the core requirements associated with large development projects.

This has consequently raised the demand level for professionals capable of analyzing and maximizing positive social impacts from real estate developments while mitigating negative effects on existing communities.

Real Estate Technology Integration

While technology is one of the major drivers of change in the real estate industry, the function of most new roles is more related to the implementation and management of those technologies than their development. Various completely new positions, like property technology implementation managers, smart building operators, or digital amenity coordinators do require organizational and communication skills rather than deep technical expertise.

The Future Of Urban Living

With the advancement of cities, their living models are just turning newer. Co-living developments, and housing across generations-integrated live-work-play communities all demand an army of managers who can manage the complexity around such living environments. Community managers, lifestyle coordinators, and residential experience designers are all going to be, or have already been, vital resources as new residential models emerge.

Investment And Financial Aspects

The sector attracts major investment in real estate and thus continues to offer diverse opportunities for professionals in the fields of real estate finance, investment analysis, and asset management. In these posts, while technical skills are rewarding, more often than not, success is based more on understanding market dynamics, building relations, and making sound judgment calls based on a variety of different factors.

Chapter Brief

Growth in the real estate and urban development sector is seeing a sea change from traditional property development and management. This evolution has come with a whole set of opportunities for a non-technical professional who can bring creativity, interpersonal skills, and strategic thinking into the process of building communities of tomorrow. As the sector continues to further evolve, professionals who can adapt to evolving needs while keeping their focus on community, sustainability, and social impact will continue to see an abundance of opportunities to carve out satisfying careers in this exciting field.

By the end of the century, the land use professions and urban development will face an urgent need for individuals able to balance the four critical priorities: environmental sustainability, social equity, economic viability, and community need. Success will depend more and more on soft skills like communication, emotional intelligence, and strategic thinking qualities beyond the reach of automation and artificial intelligence.

CHAPTER 9: LOGISTICS AND SUPPLY CHAIN

Maneuvering A New Era Of Global Commerce

The global logistics and supply chain industry has come out of recent worldwide disruptions and fundamentally changed with new priorities, challenges, and opportunities to rebuild the landscape. All this brought an unparalleled urge for professionals who can maneuver through the complexities of the modern supply chain with human oversight to create resilient operations.

E-Commerce Revolution And Its Impact

The surprise rise in e-commerce indeed overhauled traditional logistics operations by escalating demand for warehouse management professionals and distribution specialists. Highly technical automated aspects of e-commerce involve complex human judgment and leadership to keep the fulfillment operations running. Today, the warehouse manager needs to strike a balance between efficiency and flexibility, handle both automated systems and teams of people, and move with changing consumer demands.

The recent development of micro-fulfillment centers within urban areas has created a need for logistics professionals who understand not only operations management but also the dynamics of intra-urban distribution. Such professionals must now balance last-mile delivery challenges in dense urban environments with relationship management of the local community and its regulatory bodies. Therefore, skills related to route optimization, local workforce dynamics, and community relations have become as important as core logistics competencies.

Supply Chain Resilience And Risk Management

Recent global disturbances have underlined the critical need for supply chain resilience, therefore pushing up demand for professionals who can foresee and take mitigative actions against potential disturbances. Today, supply chain risk managers and resilience specialists are paramount members of any leadership team in developing sound plans for contingencies and ensuring that operations go on during times of crises.

To perform this, professionals need a delicate balance between analytics and relationship building. Data analytics can indicate the potential risk, but it is the human element in the building of strong relationships with suppliers, leveraging negotiation, and the ability to make subtle decisions in the face of complexity that determines success in managing supply chain risks.

Sustainable Logistics Operations

From peripheral concern to now, sustainability has emerged as a central priority of the logistics operation. The environmental compliance managers and sustainability coordinators are key logistics operations players whose responsibilities ensure that environmental considerations are integrated into each part of the supply chain. Professionals playing these roles need to balance environmental imperatives with operational efficiency and cost considerations.

This has given rise to the emergence of circular supply chains, which have created an avenue for managers and professionals who can competently handle reverse logistics operations and enforce sustainable packaging initiatives. Professionals specialized in this area would have to show their knowledge and skills in reducing waste, managing materials, and engaging with stakeholders by blending operational knowledge with environmental awareness and effective communication.

International Trade And Customs Management

While regionalization is a growing trend, the core of international commerce is still international trade; hence, customs brokers, trade compliance specialists, and international coordinators have fairly regular demand. Thus, it falls on them to keep up with an increasingly complicated set of international regulations while continuing to manage efficient cross-border operations.

Nowadays, trade compliance is a strategic business function that involves a deep understanding and expertise in international relations, regulatory frameworks, and risk management. A professional in the field needs to keep up with the ever-changing environment of trade agreements, sanction regimes, and customs requirements, keeping good relations with regulatory authorities and international counterparts.

Specialized Logistics Services

The growth in specialized logistics sectors has presented many opportunities for those professionals who possess expert knowledge in the handling of cargoes that are of a particular nature. Cold chain logistics, pharmaceutical distribution, and dangerous goods handling require specialists who understand both the technical requirements of these shipments and the regulatory frameworks governing their movement.

Many such roles command a premium in compensation, given the high level of responsibility and expertise involved. Ability to manage rigorous compliance standards, crisis management, and success in the execution of such tasks typically vests not only in technical knowledge but in how well one can handle the demands of the job.

Technology Integration And Human Over-Sight

While automation and artificial intelligence continue to change fundamentally how logistics operations work, human oversight and decision-making are needed now more than ever. Technology implementation managers and systems integration specialists are intricately involved in the process to ensure new technologies augment, rather than replace, human capabilities.

These professionals must narrow the gap between technical systems and human operators so that technology implementations do not hinder operational efficiency. The success behind such roles lies in driving effective change management and training in support of team members' adaptation to new systems.

Last-Mile Innovation

It has now been recognized as perhaps the most differentiating aspect of logistics operations, opening avenues for professionals who could 'think out of the box' in last-mile delivery solutions. A route optimization specialist and a delivery network manager have to balance efficiency with customer satisfaction by managing both technological tools and human delivery teams.

Urban logistics coordinators have specific challenges to face in the management of deliveries across increasingly congested city environments. In such positions creative problem-solving skills are central, and an ability to work alongside city planners, local businesses, and community stakeholders is essential. Future Trends and Opportunities

It is indeed an evolving space, and new trends open newer avenues for non-technical professionals. The fast growth of platform-based logistics services shared warehousing solutions, and collaborative delivery networks need professionals who can sort out complex partner relationships and change business models.

It is the effective integration of sustainability objectives into operational efficiency that will ensure continued opportunities for managers who can deliver green logistics solutions without necessarily compromising service quality and cost efficiency. The ability to balance the interests of multiple stakeholders while driving operational improvements remains one of the major success factors in logistics careers.

Chapter Brief

This would, of course, imply that the logistics and supply chain sector does indeed provide many opportunities for individuals to assume a leadership mantle, especially in relationship management, coupled with an appropriate level of operational acumen. The industry is indeed one in which technology remains ever-evolving, but decision-making, people skills, and crisis management will always be the domain of human resources or human capital.

Successful careers in modern logistics call for flexibility, strategic insight, and person-to-person skills all those aspects that cannot be automated. In the still further-evolving sector, satisfying opportunities will be found by professionals who can feel their way through the operational efficiency, environmental sustainability, and stakeholder management interplay.

CHAPTER 10: RETAIL AND CONSUMER GOODS

Reinventing Shopping In A Post-COVID World

The retail and consumer goods sector has seen an incredible sea change over the last few years, catalyzed by the global pandemic and shifting consumer tastes. Even while digital commerce continues to grow, the industry has seen an unexpected renaissance of human touch jobs marrying old-school retail experience with new-school consumer expectations.

The New Face Of Personal Shopping

The retail landscape has moved beyond the binary choice of online and offline, and a new generation of retail professionals has come up who are acting as personal shopping consultants cum brand ambassadors. These roles knit deep product knowledge together with emotional intelligence and personalized service delivery. Unlike recommendation automated systems, these professionals give nuanced, contextual advice that considers not just past purchases but personal style, changes in life stages, and occasions coming up in the lives of customers.

Today, many personal shoppers maintain a portfolio of clients across several channels, arranging virtual consultations but continuing to invest in face-to-face relationships. This merges into the hybrid approach that requires professionals able to move seamlessly between a digital and physical environment with consistency in service quality and personal touch.

Experiential Retail Leadership

With the onset of experiential retail, demand has opened for professionals who can curate memorable shopping experiences. The store manager becomes the experience director, tasked with the creation of immersive environments that tell compelling brand stories. These roles call for a sophisticated understanding of visual merchandising, event planning, and community engagement.

Successful experienced directors will have to balance the artistic aspects of space design against pragmatic operational requirements. Along with visual merchandisers, local artists, and community organizations, they will create dynamic store environments, which constantly change while giving customers new reasons to visit and explore stores.

Artisanal And Local Retail Management

A consequence of this is that professional opportunities have emerged for those who are able to curate unique product collections and manage local producer relationships. These merchandising specialists must balance both local market preferences and global trends while maintaining strong relationships with small-scale producers and artisans.

This work goes beyond selecting products into storytelling and community development. Indeed, professionals in this area are often involved in bringing producers and consumers closer through the organization of events, workshops, and demonstrations of local craftsmanship, strengthening social bonds within the community.

Sustainable Retail Operations

Sustainability nowadays has become a central concern in retail operations and has carved out a role for professionals who can implement and manage environmentally responsible practices in this field. Sustainability coordinators in retail settings have to balance environmental initiatives against operational efficiency and customer expectations.

These include managing recycling programs, circular fashion initiatives, coordination with sustainable suppliers, and education of staff and customers on environmental initiatives. Success requires a blend of operational experience, knowledge of the environment, and high levels of communication.

Brand Experience Integration

This is where brand experience integration across multi-channels has created the demand for professionals who can provide consistency with adaptation to channel-specific requirements. The managers have to maintain the integrity of the brand story across physical stores, online platforms, and social media, to name a few, and also in emerging channels.

This means that such roles demand an understanding of strategy in branding, together with practical skills in retail operations. Professionals will have to coordinate with digital teams while ascertaining that in-person experiences are aligned and build on the total brand narrative.

Customer Intelligence And Insights

While many retail decisions take their cue from data analytics, interpretation and application of customer insight still remain a thoroughly human task. Customer intelligence specialists use quantitative analyses in concert with qualitative understanding to distill more effective insights into consumer behavior and preference.

These professionals need to transform such data into action in the form of actionable recommendations on merchandise selection, store layout, and service delivery. Success requires much more than analytical skills in understanding and anticipating the changing needs and preferences of consumers.

Supply Chain And Inventory Management

The balance between efficiency and flexibility is crucial for today's retail supply chains, in maintaining the optimum level of inventory to satisfy the ever-changing consumer demand. The category managers and inventory specialists interact with suppliers logistics providers and store operations to ensure product availability at minimal waste.

This has been increasingly complex as omnichannel retail has fostered the requirement for a professional who can deal with inventory across different channels with profitability and sustainability in mind.

Community Engagement And Local Marketing

Community connection's growing importance to retail success has surfaced a need for professionals capable of developing and maintaining solid local relationships. Managers of community engagement will develop and execute initiatives placing stores as citizens with value to the community, rather than strictly commercial entities.

These activities include event organization in the community, local partnership management, and making stores responsive to local needs and preferences. The person would require excellent relations skills and extensive knowledge of dynamics in local marketplaces.

Emerging Trends And Changes

The retail industry keeps changing, with such emerging trends bound to create non-core opportunities for professionals within the field. Take social commerce, live shopping, and virtual retail experiences, which need professionals who can think about traditional retail skills and apply them in new formats and platforms.

With the integration of technology in retail settings, there is going to be an increase in more and more opportunities for professionals who will be able to help customers switch between digital and physical shopping. Being able to foster human connection with personal service in a highly digitized world will continue to be an important differentiator.

Chapter Brief

The transformation in retail and consumer goods has created manifold opportunities for professionals who can wed legacy retail expertise with modern-day consumer expectations. While the future of this industry will continue to be shaped by technology, at the core of retail success lie very personal elements: service, relationship, and community.

The future of retail careers is about meaningful connections: between brands and customers through bricks-and-mortar, digital, or hybrid spaces. Career opportunities abound for professionals who could innovate to meet the changing tastes and preferences of consumers, yet remain focused on personal service and commitment to the local community.

CHAPTER 11: CONSTRUCTION AND INFRASTRUCTURE

Building The Future

The global construction and infrastructure sector is at an unprecedented juncture, driven by unparalleled urbanization, sustainability imperatives, and extraordinary multibillion-dollar government investment programs across the world. With technological innovation continuing to change construction methods, success today depends increasingly on professionals capable of managing complex stakeholder relationships, and thus the human side of mega infrastructure projects.

The Global Infrastructure Renaissance

Countries around the world have initiated ambitious infrastructure renewal programs, and in the process, opened hitherto unimagined opportunities for construction management professionals. From the European Union's Green Deal, through China's Belt and Road Initiative, to the United States' Infrastructure Investment and Jobs Act, billions of public dollars are being invested in remaking the built environment. These require a professional who can coordinate intricate projects both politically and within community contexts.

While project directors and construction managers used to be responsible for the traditional processes, today they are responsible for stakeholder relations, environmental compliance, and community communications. Success in their roles is increasingly dependent on soft skills that involve diplomatic communication, cultural sensitivity, and strategic thinking.

Sustainable Construction Leadership

New roles have emerged that marry the old competencies in construction with environmental stewardship in response to the increasing demand for sustainable construction. Sustainability coordinators and green building specialists are working along with project managers who ensure construction practices meet environmental standards while sustaining project efficiency and cost-effectiveness.

These are professionals who need to balance at least four competing priorities: environmental impact, budget constraints, regulatory compliance, and project timelines. It calls for more than an understanding of sustainable building practices; it requires the ability to build consensus among a wide array of stakeholders and make convincing arguments for sustainable solutions.

Integrating Urban Planning And Development

Most of the major construction projects nowadays also demand a better integration with city planning undertakings. This leads to wider possibilities for a person who, for professionals, can bridge the gap between the construction operation and the goals of city development. Specialist integrations in urban areas work in collaboration with planners of the city, community groups, and construction teams to make sure that projects add to and do not detract from urban environments.

These are roles that involve people who can understand not only the technical aspects of construction but also social dynamics within urban settings. Success will involve facilitating dialogue between construction teams and community stakeholders and devising creative solutions to complex urban challenges.

Safety And Compliance Evolution

Construction safety and compliance have evolved beyond basic regulatory adherence to take on strategic functionality, none of which can be driven without sophisticated leadership. Today's director of safety has to build cultures of safety awareness in addition to handling increasingly complex regulatory requirements and insurance considerations.

This is accomplished through a blend of the same type of traditional safety professional with change management and applying the principles of behavioral science to make jobs safer. Today, the CSHM may also be responsible for coordinating mental health and wellness programs besides physical safety programs.

Quality Assurance And Control

Quality assurance will continue to be a strategic function given the increasing complexity of construction projects; hence, the need for professionals who can implement appropriate quality management systems. Quality directors will have to create consistency among several of the components of the project and interact with various contractors, inspectors, and regulatory agencies.
But it is not only the technical know-how that these roles demand; it is also about creating quality-focused cultures and dealing with very complex stakeholder relationships. Practitioners are often caught between multiple priorities, needing to juggle among them without sacrificing any of the quality standards.

Project Finance And Risk Management

Modern construction projects are financially complex, creating a demand for professionals who can understand the construction operation and also manage financial risk. A project finance specialist has to assess and manage risks while preserving the financial viability of projects under changing market conditions.

These are positions that call for the effective communication of required matters with financial institutions, investors, and construction teams while keeping an overview of project risks and opportunities. An increasingly valuable ability to translate between technical and financial considerations.

Supply Chain And Procurement Evolution

Construction supply chain management is increasingly becoming a strategic function of professionals charged with the responsibility of building resilient networks of suppliers while managing costs, especially sustainability imperatives. Purchasing in the construction industry involves maintaining healthy relationships with suppliers and ensuring the materials conform to increasingly stringent environmental and quality standards.

These roles require professionals who can manage global supply chains, taking up local market requirements and regulatory needs. Relationship management skills would be the key ingredient to success with an added capacity for prediction and mitigating supply chain risks.

Technology Integration Management

While the field of construction technology is constantly in development, there has been a significant growth in the demand for professionals to manage the human side of technology adoption. The technology integration manager works to bring new construction technologies in a manner that will enhance project execution and not disrupt it.

These are the roles that will require professionals to bridge the gap between technical capability and practical application and manage resistance to change while ensuring that new technologies deliver the benefits promised. Success is more dependent upon change management and communication skills than technical capability.

Community Relations And Stakeholder Management

This increasing project complexity elevates the role of stakeholder management to an integrated function that hires a full-time professional. For example, a community relations manager builds relationships with the community and ensures that project progress is not hampered.
These roles also demand that professionals can address the complex political environment, and have good relationships with different categories of stakeholders. The profession requires high communication skill levels and innovation to handle emerging community concerns.

Emerging Trends and Opportunities

In light of this, construction has embraced emerging trends that avow new opportunities for non-technical professionals. The increasing growth of modular construction, sustainable building, and integrated project delivery opens wide opportunities for induction or adapting traditional construction management skills to new contexts.

As construction projects increasingly encompass environmental and social considerations, there will continue to be opportunities for those professionals who can balance the many stakeholder interests with the drive for project success. The ability to manage complexity while staying focused on human factors will remain paramount.

Chapter Brief

Construction and infrastructure represent a huge opportunity for professionals with skill mixes that blend traditional project management expertise with modern leadership competencies. Technology may influence construction methods, yet human resources remain necessary to manage stakeholders, assess and mitigate risk, and involve communities.

It ranges from the increasingly complex nature of projects for construction careers to paying attention to sustainability, community impact, and stakeholder engagement. Those professionals who can master the challenges thrown up by them and adapt to the changing industry demands will find rewarding opportunities in this dynamic sector.

CHAPTER 12:
EXPERIENCE ECONOMY

The Future Of Personal Services

The experience economy has moved way beyond its rather modest concept to a more sophisticated ecosystem where personal services and crafted experiences co-create value in modern times. This opens a wide variety of roles for professionals who are able to create significant experiences and emotional connections in an expanding digital world.

The Emergence Of The Architecture Of Experience

Today's experience architects are challenging the paradigm of how businesses interact with customers, extending beyond service delivery into the creation of immersive, memorable experiences. Professionals combine aspects of psychology, design thinking, and cultural awareness in order to conceptualize an experience touching on an enterprise objective with personal relevance.

This means that the experience architect has to understand, in detail, human behaviors and emotional drivers of customers and, more importantly, translate these insights into tangible service experiences. Beyond conventional roles in event planning or service design, experienced architects map customer journeys to ensure every touchpoint furthers a cohesive story in some way that strengthens brand relationships.

Cultural Intelligence In Experience Design

This, in turn, has created a huge demand for cultural intelligence consultants who will help them ensure that such experiences resonate across diverse audiences. Specialists are there to lead the organization to dive into nuances of cultures, adapt experiences for different markets, and help it avoid possible cultural missteps that may crash brand reputation.

This role requires much more than knowledge of the culture; it's all about how to turn the insight into practical recommendations for designing the experience. Many of them perform the function of acting as a bridge between global brands and local markets, keeping the experiences relevant and authentic for the local audience while maintaining consistency for the brand.

Luxury Experience Evolution

In fact, the industry of luxury is truly turning from product-centric to experience-based value propositions, after all, that opens up business avenues for the luxury experience curator. These professionals actually have to balance both traditional luxury values and emerging consumer preferences in designing experiences that pay respect to heritage yet embrace innovation. Today, heritage craft revivalists play an increasingly important role in the working relationship with traditional artisans to revive and highlight historical craftsmanship relevant to the luxury consumer of today. Such a position demands profound knowledge of both craft traditions and modern luxury markets, as well as sustainability. It also calls for great sensitivity toward the balance between tradition and innovation.

Strategy Development Of Personalization

More recently, personalization strategist roles have emerged, helped by the growth in demand for experiences that are personalized. These will design and execute complex personalization programs. This requires balancing the aspiration for personalization against operational practicality, creating experiences that truly feel personalized rather than mechanically customized.

These roles demand expertise in both the realms of data analytics and human psychology: meshing quantitative insights into qualitative insights to formulate meaningful strategies for personalization. Not to forget, privacy considerations and ethical implications for which personal data must be used.

Hybrid Experience Integration

Where the lines of physical and digital experiences have blurred, so too have the requirements of professionals who are able to marry both seamlessly. Hybrid experience designers need to understand how to use technology in a manner that extends, not replaces, human-to-human interactions to build experiences that feel natural and engaging across touchpoints.

These are specialized roles that require professionals who will coordinate both digital teams and traditional experience designers, keeping the overarching customer journey in focus. Success is all about knowing when to provide enhancements with digital and when to leave well enough alone so the human elements can continue making experiences meaningful.

Community Experience Development

Community becoming more and more significant in brand building, it has opened a lot of avenues for designers in community experiences who can forge deeper connections between brands and their audiences. The said professional would have to be well-versed in group dynamics and the principles of building community to align the community experience with the brand objectives.

In community experience roles, one may be needed to handle both online and offline communities and create opportunities where meaningful interaction and experience can be shared. This will involve a high degree of emotional intelligence to develop real connections while ensuring proper boundaries.

Measurement And Impact Evaluation

The evolution of experience measurement has created roles for professionals who can assess the value of an experiential initiative beyond traditional metrics. Experience metrics analysts bring together quantitative measurement with qualitative assessment to provide a more complete picture of insight into the effectiveness of experiences.

Professions need to develop new frameworks for measuring experiential impact, translating complex data into actionable insights, demonstrating value from experiential investments, and finding opportunities for improvement.

Sustainable Experience Design

The imperative for sustainability opens up opportunities for professionals who develop environmentally responsible experiences without quality or impact compromise. In this regard, the consultants in sustainable experience need to balance the environmental considerations with the objectives of the experience and find creative solutions that enhance, rather than detract from, the customer experience.

These roles will be concerned with liaising with suppliers, venues, and service providers on the delivery of sustainable practice, often without compromising high levels of service delivery. There is a growing need for expertise in environmental issues combined with the ability to make sustainability both relevant and interesting to customers.

Future Trends And Innovations

The experience economy is in continuous evolution, as emergent trends create new directions for innovation in personal services. Growth in immersive technologies, wellness experiences, and purpose-driven programming demands a professional able to adapt traditional principles in experience design to new contexts.

It, therefore, calls for successful professionals to advance, developing their sense in relation to the shifting consumer preferences while still maintaining a focus on the human elements that make experiences meaningful. In so doing, the capability to balance innovation with authenticity in the continuous evolution of the sector shall be cardinal.

Chapter Brief

The experience economy is indeed very lucrative, allowing ample opportunities for professionals who can combine emotional intelligence with strategic thinking in order to create experiences. While technology might have opened up newer avenues of delivering experiences, the human elements of empathy, creativity, and personal connection are at the heart of any successful experience.

The future of experience design will be about creating authentic, meaningful connections with others in a world where digital is increasingly at the forefront. Those professionals who can rise to this challenge in concert with changing consumer preferences and imperatives of sustainability are the ones who get truly rewarded through this dynamic sector.

CHAPTER 13: AGRICULTURE AND FOOD PRODUCTION

Global Non-Technology Employment's Backbone

Agriculture and food production remain one of the pivots of employment generation globally, taking care of the livelihoods of millions and fulfilling one of the most basic needs of human food. While for many industries the rulebook is being rewritten due to rapid advances in technology, agriculture remains a mainstay of employment generation in at least non-technology-intensive economies. The chapter brings out the changing contours of agriculture and food production, the drivers and inhibitors of employment generation, and the possibility of sustainable, high-output employment in this vital sector.

Agricultural Employment:

A Global Perspective Employment attributable to agriculture is highly irregularly dispersed geographically, climatically, and economically. In the less developed parts of the world, it often employs a very high percentage of the labor force. In many African and Southeast Asian countries, for instance, the share can be as high as 60% of all jobs and is often the leading sector in those economies. On the other hand, although agriculture is less extensively employed in developed countries, it still plays an important role in the rural economy of towns and is the main source of employment where urbanization is limited.

Agricultural jobs span traditional areas, including farming and animal husbandry to a variety of niche specialist opportunities in food safety, agronomy, and urban agriculture. As the industry diversifies-integrating new methods its job functions evolve to include career opportunities with emphases on sustainable practices in managing soil health, regenerative farming, and organic food production. These changes do suggest an industry playing its role to meet environmental imperatives and market demands, but also one reinforcing its role as a job creator.

Forces Behind Agricultural Employment Growth

Growing population, urbanization, and increase in consumer preference are driving agriculture and food production. Food demand globally is expected to increase by 60% in 2050, while an increasing population and changes in diets take the lead, especially in developing economies where people can increasingly afford a wide array of high-quality foods. This demand fuels job creation across the food production supply chain, from farming to processing, distribution, and sales.

Moreover, the movement toward sustainable agriculture propels job growth. As more and more consumers are seeking out transparency in how their food is grown, most agricultural operations must shift toward more sustainable practices, in turn creating new competencies such as environmental science, organic certification, and resource management. The rising demand for agricultural professionals competent to perform these growing demands underpins the movement of this industry from traditional farming into a value-added, knowledge-based industry.

Key Job Openings In Agriculture And Food Production

1. Farmers and Crop Managers: These professions represent the backbone of agricultural production in the growth of food, feed, and fiber. Today's farmer, with the advancement in crop management and conservation of resources, has to incorporate traditional skills with modern agronomic knowledge. Additional training in sustainable methods and environmental stewardship could enhance these professions to meet productivity with ecological responsibility.

2. Agronomists/Soil Scientists: With agriculture taking a different turn toward regenerative methods, agronomists and soil scientists are gaining great demand. They optimize the health of the soils, which are considered the epicenter of sustainable crop production. This ranges from analyzing the composition of the soil to advising on crop rotation and designing methods of erosion control with the least use of chemicals. Soil health is at the heart of resilient agriculture; thus, the area specialists make a critical contribution to the development of sustainable methods.

3. Food Safety Inspectors: Due to the worldwide supply chains that move food products from farm to table often over great distances, this has been an increasingly important job in ensuring the safety of foodstuffs. Food safety inspectors ensure standards for food safety are followed, supporting health requirements both locally and through imports. The increase in health-conscious consumerism supports this need for professionals within the food production ecosystem.

4. Urban Farm Developers and Vertical Farming Specialists: With urban farming picking up the pace in several cities globally, a considerable part of their fresh produce is grown closer to the consumers. This opens possibilities for managing urban farms, vertical farming, and hydroponics. These specialists develop high-density and efficient ways of production to solve food security in cities. It is also seen as a means of reducing carbon footprint from the transportation of food, besides returning jobs to the heart of the cities.

Issues Affecting Agriculture And Food Production

Some of the major issues affecting agriculture and food production, which directly implicate employment, are climate change, fluctuating prices of commodities, and labor shortages. Of all these, the gravest would probably be climate change due to its erratic change in weather, unexpected droughts, and the degradation of the soil that affects crop yield and farming conditions. Adaptation implies investment in technology, dissemination of knowledge, and government support to protect employment and assure productivity in agriculture.

Labor shortages hamper the performance of farm enterprises, particularly in the case of developed countries. Farm work is very labor-intensive, and with rural depopulation, fewer people want to work in agriculture. Various governments and industry organizations assist in promoting training programs that prepare a young population with agricultural skills, while other initiatives focus on easing labor conditions as encouragement for more individuals to join the profession.

This, in turn, affects the stability of agricultural jobs. When commodity prices fall, the farmer receives lower returns, which means lower job security for the agricultural worker. High prices create incentives to expand, although such growth is often dampened by increasing production costs. Agricultural professionals must balance economic viability with sustainable practices in order to protect jobs and resources amid these ups and downs.

Sustainable Agriculture And The Future Of Employment

Agriculture has shifted to green technologies in this age where sustainability is first, therefore opening more avenues for green job professions within the sector. Sustainable agriculture takes into consideration three important features: soil health, water conservation, and biodiversity. All these need expertise that has been trained in environmental management. The shift towards organic farming, permaculture, and agroforestry opens different positions for employment.

Agricultural education equips the next generation of farmers with sustainable practices. Agricultural universities and vocational training facilities increasingly reflect courses on environmental science and technology that foster a workforce that is attuned to the unique needs of sustainable agriculture. Governments and organizations also promote these various programs with many offering subsidies and incentives for young people to take up agricultural careers

Agriculture's Role In A Non-Integrated Job Market

Agriculture remains one of the most resilient job providers for an increasingly changing economy. While most industries are finding further integrated uses of technology, agriculture remains one of the holdouts in terms of non-integrated jobs that require people-to-people skills and hands-on expertise. Its ability to adapt to urban agriculture, sustainable methods, and other such needs of society goes a long way in showing just how the industry can change with the times-without sacrificing its function of providing valuable jobs.

In the future, job generation and the retention of jobs by agriculture are related to its meeting of environmental, economic, and social challenges. New opportunities for employment, according to new trends, would be opened by the shift toward sustainable agriculture, the growth of urban farming, and higher standards for food safety. Agriculture will continue to hold a top rank in employment patterns in developed and developing areas so long as the activity remains basic to human life at the core of the prosperity and stability of the world.

CHAPTER 14: TOP 30 INDUSTRIES CREATING MOST NON-TECHNOLOGY JOBS IN THE NEXT DECADE

1. **Healthcare Services**
   - Jobs: Nursing, physical therapy, medical assisting, and public health administration.
   - Key Drivers: Aging populations, rising healthcare demands, and increased focus on wellness.

2. **Elderly and Home Care**
   - Jobs: Assisted living staff, home healthcare aides, and geriatric care managers.
   - Key Drivers: Growing elderly population and preference for in-home care services.

3. **Wellness and Preventative Health**
   - Jobs: Nutritionists, holistic health coaches, fitness trainers, mental wellness counselors.
   - Key Drivers: Public emphasis on proactive health and mental wellness.

4. **Education and Training**

- Jobs: Teachers, corporate trainers, curriculum designers, vocational educators.
- Key Drivers: Increasing demand for lifelong learning, upskilling, and educational access.

5. **Environmental and Sustainability Services**
   - Jobs: Sustainability consultants, recycling coordinators, waste management specialists.
   - Key Drivers: Global sustainability goals, climate action, and environmental policies.

6. **Green Construction and Sustainable Building**
   - Jobs: Eco-friendly construction managers, sustainable material specialists, green certification consultants.
   - Key Drivers: Shift toward sustainable infrastructure and eco-conscious real estate development.

7. **Hospitality, Travel, and Tourism**
   - Jobs: Hotel managers, adventure tourism guides, eco-tourism planners, wellness retreat staff.
   - Key Drivers: Rebound in global tourism, demand for unique travel experiences, and sustainable tourism.

8. **Retail and Consumer Goods**
   - Jobs: Customer service representatives, merchandisers, supply chain managers.
   - Key Drivers: Persistent demand in physical retail, personalized shopping experiences.

9. **Real Estate and Property Management**
   - Jobs: Property managers, leasing consultants, real estate developers.
   - Key Drivers: Urbanization, residential demand, and the growth of mixed-use developments.

10. **Public Sector and Government Services**
   - Jobs: Urban planners, policy developers, public health officials, municipal services staff.
   - Key Drivers: Public infrastructure demands, urban planning needs, and local government growth.

11. **Nonprofits and NGOs**
   - Jobs: Fundraisers, community outreach coordinators, program managers.
   - Key Drivers: Increasing public awareness on social issues, global humanitarian needs.

12. **Logistics and Supply Chain Management**
   - Jobs: Warehouse managers, logistics coordinators, inventory analysts.
   - Key Drivers: E-commerce boom, supply chain resilience, global trade dynamics.

13. **Agriculture and Food Production**
   - Jobs: Farmers, agronomists, food safety inspectors, urban farm developers.
   - Key Drivers: Rising food demand, sustainable agriculture, and food security.

14. Food Services and Culinary Arts

- Jobs: Chefs, restaurant managers, catering coordinators, artisanal food producers.
- Key Drivers: Culinary innovation, demand for unique dining experiences, food entrepreneurship.

15. Personal Care Services

- Jobs: Hairdressers, skincare specialists, massage therapists.
- Key Drivers: Expanding wellness industry, emphasis on self-care and beauty services.

16. Arts, Entertainment, and Recreation

- Jobs: Performing artists, museum staff, event coordinators, recreational instructors.
- Key Drivers: Continued demand for creative expression, leisure, and live entertainment.

17. Childcare and Early Childhood Education

- Jobs: Daycare providers, preschool teachers, child development specialists.
- Key Drivers: Increased awareness of early childhood education benefits, dual-income households.

18. Fitness and Recreational Services

- Jobs: Personal trainers, fitness instructors, sports managers.
- Key Drivers: Focus on health and fitness, recreational sports popularity.

19. Security and Public Safety

- Jobs: Private security guards, emergency managers, disaster response coordinators.
- Key Drivers: Growing emphasis on safety, disaster preparedness, and community security.

20. Transportation Services

- Jobs: Public transit operators, logistics planners, delivery service providers.
- Key Drivers: Urban transportation growth, global delivery demand, last-mile delivery.

21. Waste Management and Recycling

- Jobs: Waste collectors, recycling plant operators, environmental cleanup crews.
- Key Drivers: Environmental policies, sustainable waste practices, circular economy trends.

22. Animal Care and Veterinary Services

- Jobs: Veterinary technicians, animal shelter workers, pet groomers, trainers.
- Key Drivers: Rising pet ownership, increased focus on animal welfare.

23. Funeral and End-of-Life Services

- Jobs: Funeral directors, grief counselors, end-of-life planners.
- Key Drivers: Aging population, need for compassionate end-of-life services.

24. Event Planning and Coordination

- Jobs: Event planners, corporate event coordinators, wedding organizers.
- Key Drivers: Demand for unique events, social gatherings, and corporate functions.

25. Insurance Services

- Jobs: Claims processors, underwriters, policy managers, customer support.
- Key Drivers: Growing insurance awareness, diversified insurance products, risk management.

26. Agritourism and Local Food Markets

- Jobs: Farm-tour coordinators, market vendors, community-supported agriculture organizers.
- Key Drivers: Demand for local foods, farm-to-table movement, sustainable farming exposure.

27. Automotive Maintenance and Repair

- Jobs: Mechanics, repair technicians, auto service advisors.
- Key Drivers: Longevity of personal vehicles, rise in electric and hybrid vehicle maintenance needs.

28. Legal and Mediation Services

- Jobs: Paralegals, mediation specialists, legal administrators.
- Key Drivers: Increasing legal service needs, rise in mediation over litigation.

29. Social Work and Community Services

- Jobs: Social workers, family counselors, community outreach professionals.
- Key Drivers: Increased social support needs, mental health awareness, youth support services.

30. Janitorial and Building Maintenance

- Jobs: Facility managers, custodians, groundskeepers.
- Key Drivers: Demand for clean, safe workspaces, facility upkeep, growth in commercial real estate.

Insights Of Our Recommendations

- **Human-Centric Roles**: Many jobs in these industries rely on interpersonal skills, empathy, and direct interaction, creating resilience against full automation.
- **Sustainability and Wellness**: Sectors focused on sustainability, health, and community support continue to grow due to global shifts in values.
- **Essential and Resilient Services**: These roles serve fundamental human needs that remain consistent across different economies, making them stable and adaptable globally.

ACKNOWLEDGEMENT

The ideas in this book represent more than two decades of professional life supported by hundreds of people who touched my path along the way. To all those who have helped in any way, I would like to extend my most profound appreciation to each of them.

To my professional colleagues and mentors throughout my career, your mentorship and shared experiences mean more than words can express. The relationships we have built in the various projects and challenges form the backbone of many of the lessons detailed within these pages.

I also remain especially grateful to my team members over the years, particularly to those young professionals who bring fresh thinking into each and every project that I work on. Your questions, your insights, and your drive to get things done still inspire me to be a better leader. It also provided many of the pragmatic recommendations you will find throughout this book.

Lastly, to my wife, Biyu, your encouragement and unabating support have been an anchor for me in each challenging moment that came my professional way. To my family members, who have stood by me through the long hours at work and stressful periods, thanks for your understanding; it has formed the bedrock of my journey so far.

While the words are mine, the wisdom they contain belongs to all who have shaped my professional life. The merits of this book are a direct reflection of the exceptional global network while any shortcomings or drawbacks are entirely my own responsibility.

ABOUT THE AUTHOR

Stephan S Sunn

Stephan Sunn is the Executive Partner at Sanford Black Advisory, a preeminent global business and investment consultancy. In this capacity, he collaborates with industry leaders to advise companies worldwide on growth strategy, marketing/sales, innovation monetization, partnerships, and mergers & acquisitions. Over the past two decades, Mr. Sunn has consulted on sourcing provider selection for more than 30 international corporations and over 20 investment and M&A deals in the technology services, digital technologies, and global outsourcing sectors.

Mr. Sunn possesses particular expertise in empowering private enterprises to accelerate growth and enhance value creation through engagement with governments and technology parks. He holds a leadership position with Devott Co., China's largest private research firm focused on the IT, software, and technology services industries. Additionally, he serves as a Director at the China IT and Outsourcing Association. His clients span Fortune 500 companies, state-owned enterprises, technology parks, SMBs, and startups in both developed and emerging markets.

A graduate of the University of Science and Technology of China (USTC) with a Bachelor of Science degree, and Yale University with a Master of Science and Ph.D., Mr. Sunn frequently shares his insights and research as a speaker at global conferences and events. He is a prolific author and an accomplished presenter for his projects and clients around the world.

BOOKS BY THIS AUTHOR

Competing For The Growth:
How Cities And Technology Parks Attract Global Trades And
Investments

This book serves as a guidebook for city planners, economic development professionals, tech park builders, and public officials who aim to create thriving innovation communities that attract global trade and stimulate investments. It offers a structured path that begins with intangible factors like vision setting and partnership alignment and extends to pilots and full-blown magnet programs.

The book provides real-life instructions to help put these ideas into practice, including effective strategies for attracting rapidly growing businesses and talent, creating a setting that promotes innovation and entrepreneurship, fostering a competitive and appealing business climate, and building a globally recognized brand and reputation.

The author emphasizes that cities and tech parks must play to their strengths and assets to compete and win in the global arena. The race for relevance is on, and the window of opportunity to determine the outcome is closing. Cities and companies have what they need to succeed, and with the options, relationships, and guidance provided in this book, city managers and tech park authorities can make the decisions necessary to lead their communities to success in the world investment and trade arena.

Searching The New Profits:
How The US SMEs And Startups Succeed In The Emerging Markets

In the face of global market turbulence and domestic uncertainties, American small and medium-sized businesses (SMBs) and startups have significant growth opportunities in emerging markets. However, these markets also present unique challenges. This handbook provides a semi-analytical and semi-prescriptive approach to help American SMBs and entrepreneurs succeed in these rapidly expanding markets. Conversely, governments, technology parks, and corporations in emerging countries can utilize this book to learn how to collaborate with U.S. companies in their markets to serve their customers effectively.

The book covers essential themes such as researching and identifying matching markets, choosing the appropriate market entry mode, local marketing and sales tactics, effective risk management, establishing an active and reputable presence in the local market, ensuring full legal compliance, avoiding political involvement, talent search and retention, and balancing standardization and localization. The final chapter shares valuable lessons from decades of business practices, acknowledging that readers may have different perspectives on these topics. Expanding knowledge through diverse viewpoints is beneficial for U.S. SMB and startup leaders. Despite the challenges, penetrating foreign markets can be highly profitable, and U.S. enterprises have a reasonable chance of success by capitalizing on the vast potential of these rapidly growing territories.

Cracking The Winning Codes:
How Global Vendors Win In The US Digital And Outsourcing Markets

This book serves as a comprehensive guide for international technology and outsourcing companies seeking to enter and succeed in the highly competitive U.S. market. It emphasizes the importance of adapting to the unique American business culture, which values innovation, diversity, relationships, customer-centricity, and results-oriented management. The guide highlights the need to navigate the complex U.S. regulatory landscape, including federal and state laws, as well as key legislations such as FCPA, SOX, and HIPAA.

The book covers essential topics such as understanding American business culture, complying with legal requirements, developing effective marketing strategies, employing successful sales techniques, addressing cultural differences, and managing risks associated with entering a new market. Additionally, it encourages the use of innovative tactics to differentiate from competitors and gain market share.

A special section titled "The Lessons" shares the author's personal experiences and insights, providing practical execution tips that focus on solution-oriented approaches, leveraging referrals and testimonials, managing communication costs, delivering higher quality than promised, and investing in proven local sales leaders.

By adhering to the core principles of understanding buyer preferences, continuous innovation, human capital development, risk management, customer-centricity, and resilient operations, global providers can successfully navigate and thrive in the lucrative U.S. market.

Emerging Niche Industries
High-Growth Sectors Of The Future Jobs

The book "Emerging 50 Niche Industries – High-Growth Sectors of Future Jobs" provides a roadmap for professionals seeking lucrative careers in specialized industries poised for significant expansion. It begins by highlighting the paradigm shift in career success, emphasizing adaptability, continuous learning, and the alignment of passion with prosperity as crucial to thriving in a dynamic job market. Traditional career paths are contrasted with niche careers, which allow for rapid growth, cross-border opportunities, and high earning potential in unique, underserved fields. Key areas of exploration include emerging technologies, such as artificial intelligence, cybersecurity, and biotechnology, which drive demand for highly specialized roles. The book also delves into the creative economy, where digital content creation and online education offer unprecedented monetization avenues, and sustainability sectors like renewable energy, food tech, and green building, which are critical in addressing global environmental challenges.

Additionally, the text addresses the financial sector's evolution through fintech, digital assets, and ESG investing, where professionals can shape sustainable investment trends. Niche opportunities in luxury markets and healthcare innovation also showcase high-reward roles for those with specialized skills and global perspectives.

For aspiring professionals, the book advocates for interdisciplinary skills, ethical considerations, and a global mindset as essential strategies for excelling in niche industries that balance wealth creation with meaningful, future-focused impact.

Asian Startup Failures:
Lessons And Case Studies For Success

The book "Failures of Asian Startups: Key Lessons and Case Studies" examines the reasons for startup failures across Asia, emphasizing challenges stemming from internal dynamics, the broader Asian business environment, and country-specific factors. The book categorizes common failures into several themes, such as strategic misalignment, financial mismanagement, leadership struggles, and market entry challenges.

One prominent theme is the difficulty startups face in scaling operations due to Asia's diverse regulatory landscapes and fragmented markets, where cultural nuances and regulatory differences often hinder consistent growth. Many startups fail by adopting Western business models without adequate localization, leading to poor customer adoption and operational setbacks. Additionally, excessive reliance on venture capital for rapid scaling often pressures startups into unsustainable growth practices, such as high customer acquisition costs without a focus on retention, undermining long-term viability.

Through detailed case studies, including companies like Honestbee, Zilingo, and Ofo, the book underscores the importance of local adaptability, sustainable unit economics, and resilient operational models. It advocates for strategies like in-depth market research, localization, and balancing growth with profitability to foster sustainable success. By learning from these common pitfalls, the next generation of Asian entrepreneurs can build more resilient and culturally attuned businesses for the complex and dynamic Asian markets

Top 50 Job-Creating Industries Of The Next Decade

The book, titled Top 50 Job-Creating Industries of the Next Decade by Stephan S. Sunn and his partners, details the industries of the future that are going to dominate the era of employment generation. Sunn focuses on the main drivers: technology, healthcare, and sustainability. He further drills down into sectors such as artificial intelligence, digital transformation, green economy, and healthcare innovation. It has also been pointed out that each sector will create diverse jobs - from data scientists and cybersecurity experts to planners of green infrastructure and consultants in telemedicine.

He first shows the required skills and transitions within economies by elaborating on industry trends, including automation, global trading shifts, and the gig economy. Of course, this book also stresses pragmatically that lifelong learning, adaptability, and digital literacy will be necessary to cope with the constant evolution of the job market. The book will be structured to help students, career changers, and entrepreneurs sail through the modern job market by offering them a realistic look at how they could position themselves within these emerging industries.

Top 20 Startup Ideas To Watch In 2024 -2026

The book "Top 20 Start-up Ideas for 2024-2026" reviews different opportunities that entrepreneurs are opening their businesses in several fast-changing industries, driven by global technological, social, and economic trends. It begins with a glimpse into the changes in the startup space: digital transformation, hybrid work, Defi-all turbocharged by the pandemic. It argues that all these are unique entry points into business.

Each of the chapters describes certain industries and names more concrete startup ideas, technologies that could be in demand, and possible challenges. AI-powered healthcare would require predictive analytics, personalized health platforms, and mental health tech from startups. Climate tech ventures are encouraged to create solutions around carbon capture, supply chain transparency, and green investments all pressing needs of the environment. The "Future of Work" sector calls for tools to be built for remote collaboration, skills-based hiring, and workplace wellness.

Other exciting industries are fintech, including embedded finance and DeFi; smart cities; education technology; agriculture, food technology, all described and dealt with recommendations about their future development. Besides this, it underlines consumer technology, virtual and augmented reality, and autonomous vehicles as a direction where immersive experience and sustainability will make ground for demand in the future. Blockchain and

Web3 companies, potentially able to change trust and ownership in a decentralized way, are discussed.

It finally drives home the need for strategic planning, adaptability, and resilience in building a "future-proof" startup. The book encourages innovation, compliance with the laws of the land, and cultural adaptability as ways to penetrate dynamically changing global markets. This guide is, therefore, a complete comprehensive roadmap for emerging entrepreneurs in 2024-2026